Virtual Reality

Beyond the Looking Glass

Produced in cooperation with

WTTW Chicago

and

Kurtis Productions, Ltd.

Adapted by

Elaine Pascoe

A BLACKBIRCH PRESS BOOK
WOODBRIDGE, CONNECTICUT

C.1 1998 10.50

Published by Blackbirch Press, Inc.
260 Amity Road
Woodbridge, CT 06525

web site: http://www.blackbirch.com
email: staff@blackbirch.com

For WTTW Chicago
Edward Menaker, Executive Producer
For Kurtis Productions, Ltd.
Bill Kurtis, Executive Producer

First Edition

Printed in the United States of America

10 9 8 7 6 5 4 3 2 1

Library of Congress Cataloging-in-Publication Data

Pascoe, Elaine.
Virtual reality : beyond the looking glass / by Elaine Pascoe.
p. cm. — (New explorers)
Includes bibliographical references and index.
Summary: Discusses in general terms the computer technology involved in virtual reality and how it has been used and will be used in the future.
ISBN 1-56711-228-5 (lib. bdg. : alk. paper)
1. Human-computer interaction—Juvenile literature. 2. Virtual reality—Juvenile literature. [1. Virtual reality] I. Title. II. Series.
QA76.9.H85P375 1998
006—dc20 96-42984
CIP
AC

Introduction

In 1990, I was lucky enough to help create a very special new "club." Its members come from all corners of the earth and are of all ages. They can be found braving crowded cities, floating among brilliantly colored coral reefs, and scaling desolate mountaintops. We call these people "New Explorers" because—in one way or another—they seek to uncover important knowledge or travel to places that others merely dream of.

No matter where they are, or what they do, New Explorers dedicate their lives to expanding the horizons of their science. Some are biologists. Others are physicists, neurosurgeons, or ethnobotanists. Still others are engineers, teachers, even cave divers. Each of them has worked hard to push limits—to go the extra step in the pursuit of a truly significant discovery.

In his quest for a breakthrough, Mike Madden is a typical New Explorer. For eight years, he was obsessed with proving that a 27-mile (44-kilometer) underwater cave system was actually connected to the Caribbean Sea. To do this, Madden swam through tunnels never before traveled by humans. Each dive was a calculated risk—a very great one—but well worth it, for Madden also proved this was the longest underwater cave system in the world.

Madden's story, like those of all the New Explorers, is what science is all about. Science is about adventure. It's about curiosity and discovery. And, sometimes, science is also about danger.

New Explorers make it clear that science is not confined to laboratories or classrooms. They show us that science is all around us; it's at the dark and frigid bottom of our oceans, it's inside an atom, it's light-years away in a galaxy we've yet to discover. My goal—and that of this series—is to travel along with people who are pursuing the seemingly impossible, journeying into the unknown. We want to be there as scientists and innovators make their discoveries. And we want you to be part of the process of discovery as well.

Accompanying these bold and courageous individuals—and documenting their work—has not been a simple task. When Mike Madden finally made his breakthrough, I—and the New Explorers camera crew—was there in the water with him. Over the years, I have also climbed into eagles' nests, tracked a deadly virus, cut my way through thick South American rain forests, trekked deep into East Africa's Masai territory, and flown jet fighters high above the clouds with some of the U.S. Air Force's most fearless Top Guns.

As you witness the achievements we bring you through New Explorers books, you may start thinking that most of the world's great discoveries have already been made, that all the great frontiers have already been explored. But nothing could be further from the truth. In fact, scientists and researchers are now uncovering more uncharted frontiers than ever before.

As host and executive producer of our television program, my mission is to find the most fascinating and exciting New Explorers of our time. I hope that their adventures will inspire you to undertake adventures of your own—to seek out and be curious, to find answers and contemplate or create solutions. At the very best, these stories will turn you into one of the world's Newest Explorers—the men and women who will capture our imaginations and thrill us with discoveries well into the 21st century.

Bill Kurtis

Bill Kurtis

We are at the edge of the 21st century, and it has happened: Mind and machine have merged to create a new world...inside the computer.

Hello, I'm Bill Kurtis. When most of us hear the words "virtual reality," we think of games—games in which the player is totally immersed in an interactive, computerized world. But today, researchers are probing and expanding a new world of virtual reality. As they probe, they try to push and expand the boundaries of computer technology to see what its limitations are—if there are limitations.

In this NEW EXPLORERS journey, we're going to leave the world of games. We'll follow these researchers to a place where virtual reality is used as an incredible tool of science and learning, a tool that could change exploration forever.

7 *Virtual Reality*

A Tool of Science

We're at the campus of the University of North Carolina (UNC), where basketball star Michael Jordan went to school. It's an ordinary day of learning here. Or is it? Students are going to class. But instead of a pencil and paper, some students are using a helmet and trigger. They're studying virtual reality, or VR—all in the name of science.

UNC has the leading virtual reality research facility in he United States. Dr. Fred Brooks started the computer science department here in 1964. In 1978, Dr. Henry Fuchs joined him. Both scientists had been excited about virtual reality since the late 1960s, so there was an instant match.

A special helmet and hand-held trigger are used to experience the virtual world.

Today, with a staff of computer scientists and students, they've built their own virtual reality system to use as a tool for scientific exploration. The system is truly amazing. Among other things, it can help chemists visualize atoms, which are too small to be viewed, even under the most powerful microscope. Virtual reality technology can even help surgeons see inside a "virtual" human body.

"Computer scientists are toolsmiths," says Brooks. "The computer's ability to help surgeons with their procedures, to help scientists understand their data, to help chemists understand how to design drugs better—I think these have the greatest potential for helping people."

If computers can do these things, Brooks and his co-workers believe, virtual reality is the way in which it will be done. Only virtual reality offers a view of a three-dimensional, computer-generated world, allowing you to see every corner, every detail, as if you'd actually stepped inside.

UNC researcher Dr. Warren Robinett explains: "My take on the whole field of virtual reality is that it's a way to expand human perception, to let you see the invisible. It can transport you to distant places, and let you see what surrounds you and talk to people there. It can transport you into microscopic worlds. It lets you perceive things that you cannot perceive with your built-in senses. In a way, you're 'boldly going where no man has gone before.'"

Dr. Fred Brooks: "Mind and Machine Together"

"I was 13 years old when I read in a magazine—in the small town in eastern North Carolina, where I grew up—about the Harvard Mark I computer that Howard Aiken had built," recalls UNC researcher Dr. Fred Brooks. The Mark I, built in 1944, was the first large-scale, fully

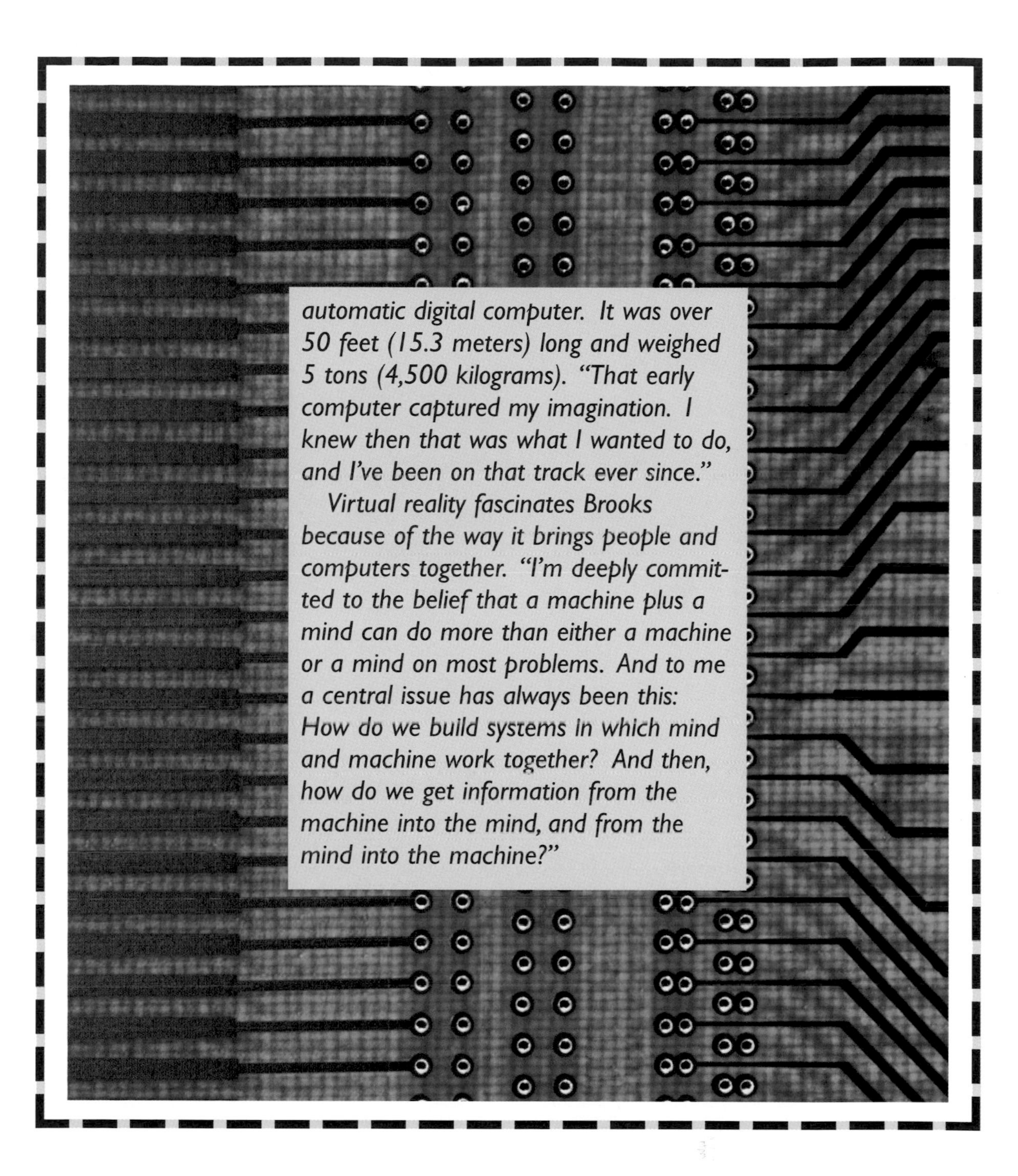

automatic digital computer. It was over 50 feet (15.3 meters) long and weighed 5 tons (4,500 kilograms). "That early computer captured my imagination. I knew then that was what I wanted to do, and I've been on that track ever since."

Virtual reality fascinates Brooks because of the way it brings people and computers together. "I'm deeply committed to the belief that a machine plus a mind can do more than either a machine or a mind on most problems. And to me a central issue has always been this: How do we build systems in which mind and machine work together? And then, how do we get information from the machine into the mind, and from the mind into the machine?"

Inside Virtual Reality

Here's how the UNC virtual reality "tool" works: The system begins with a sophisticated computer program. It can produce three-dimensional graphics in what is called "real time;" that is, a new picture is displayed every 30 seconds, so the view is constantly updated.

UNC researcher Dr. Warren Robinett sees virtual reality as a powerful tool for scientific exploration.

"Virtual reality is a way to expand human perception."

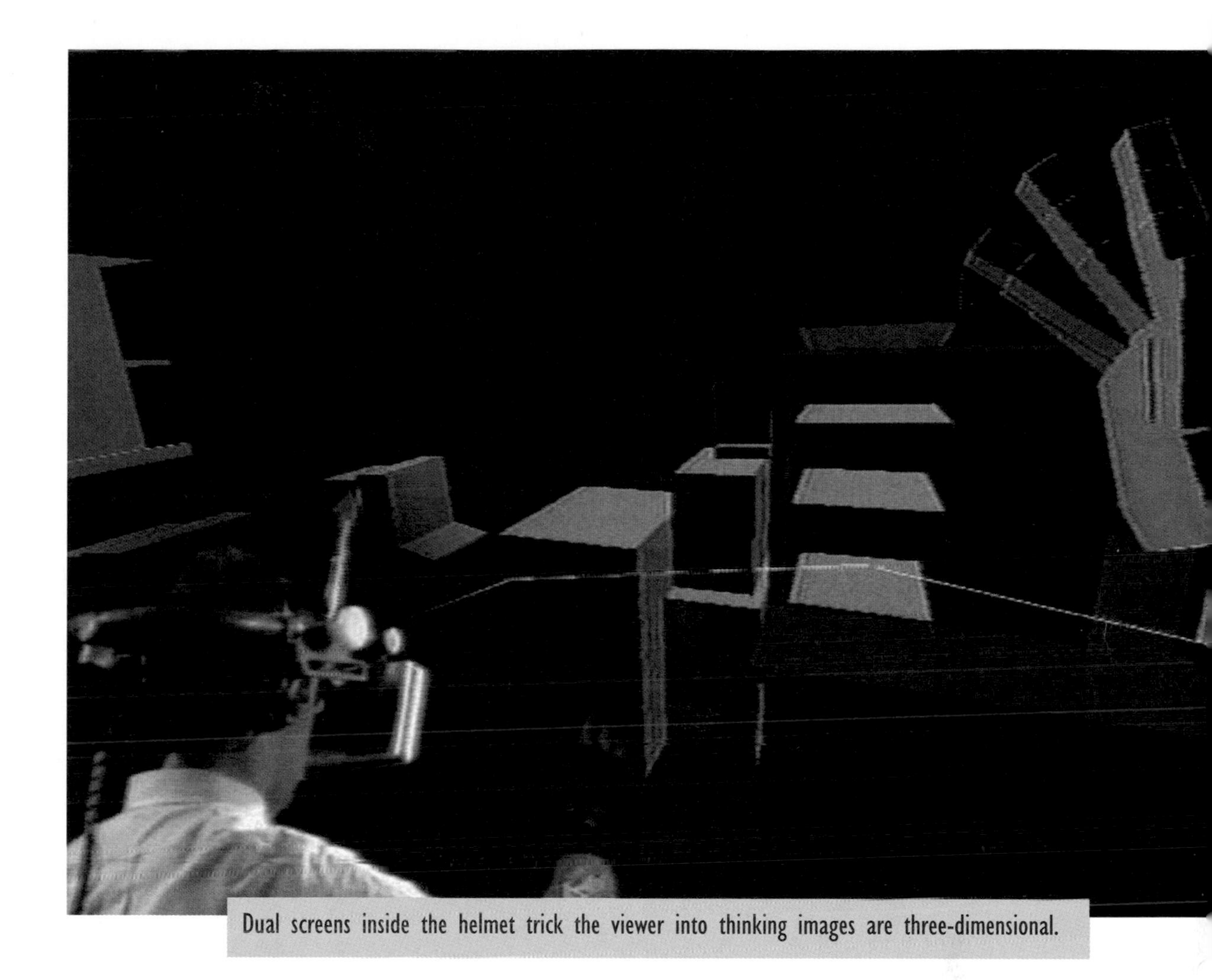

Dual screens inside the helmet trick the viewer into thinking images are three-dimensional.

Users see the images through a head-mounted display, a sort of helmet. It houses two small television screens—one for each eye. The dual screens trick your eyes, so that you think you're looking into a three-dimensional world. As you turn your head, a sensor on the top of the helmet tracks your head movements. It tells the computer what pictures to generate, so that your view changes when you look up, down, or to the side.

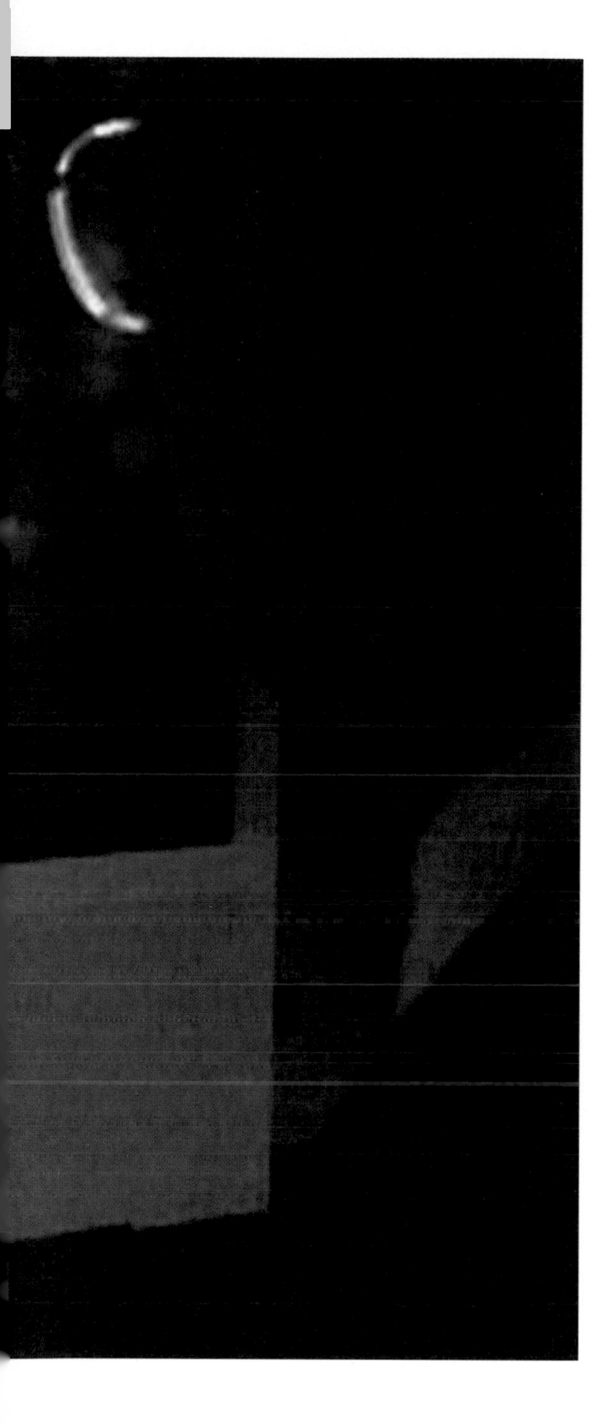

At the UNC research center, VR users join Dr. Henry Fuchs for their voyages into virtual reality. Bill Kurtis describes his first experience this way:

> *Wearing the head-mounted display, I float through a field of colored balls—three-dimensional computer-generated images of molecules. Moving around and under the molecules is almost like scuba diving on a coral reef. Next, I do some virtual artwork, using a hand-held trigger to construct a box and create a three-dimensional design with virtual "shaving cream."*
>
> *What's it like in virtual reality? I feel sort of like a ghost—weightless, able to walk through walls, fly at will, go wherever I can dream.*

Dr. Henry Fuchs is one of the world's leading virtual reality pioneers.

Into a Virtual World

The exciting new world of virtual reality started in the 1960s with a computer scientist named Ivan Sutherland. He believed that the computer should be able to create images that look, sound, and feel real enough to draw the user inside. People who design computer graphics, he thought, should think of the computer screen as a window into a virtual world. That led him to the idea of the head-mounted display, which puts the cyberspace images right in front of your eyes and immerses you in the world created by the computer.

Sutherland's work was largely ignored for years. Says Fuchs: "If you look in standard textbooks on interactive computer graphics from the 1980s, Ivan Sutherland's work on head-mounted displays is put in a paragraph in the back. Nobody realized that this was one of the major branches of interactive computer graphics. It was relegated to the dust heap."

Other scientists worked on virtual reality over the next 20 years. But it wasn't until the video-game craze of the 1980s that its enormous entertainment capabilities were discovered. A dreadlocked computer whiz-kid named Jaron Lanier became a leader in the field. He designed a system in which users wear a "data glove," a glove packed with sensors that telegraph hand movements to the computer. With the data glove, a person can reach out and touch, even move, objects that exist only in the virtual world.

Early developments in virtual reality took place in the 1960s.

A computer scientist named Ivan Sutherland was the first to envision a computer-created world that would be experienced with a headset.

How It Works

Virtual reality begins with a powerful computer that creates complex three-dimensional graphics. What really sets a VR system apart from other computer imaging systems, though, is the fact that you don't just view the graphics. You become part of the virtual world, surrounded by the images and interacting with them.

Such interaction is made possible by special equipment. In most VR systems, users wear special headgear, in the form of goggles or a helmet. This headgear is called a head-mounted display (HMD). The computer transmits images to two tiny video screens in the HMD, one for each eye. The images are just slightly different for the right eye and the left eye, and this creates the illusion of depth. Old-fashioned stereopticons and the latest 3-D films use the same trick. You're fooled into thinking that you're in the middle of a three-dimensional world.

Sensors are another key component. You can interact with the virtual

Head-mounted sensors, tiny video screens, and computer imaging enable users to truly interact with the images they see.

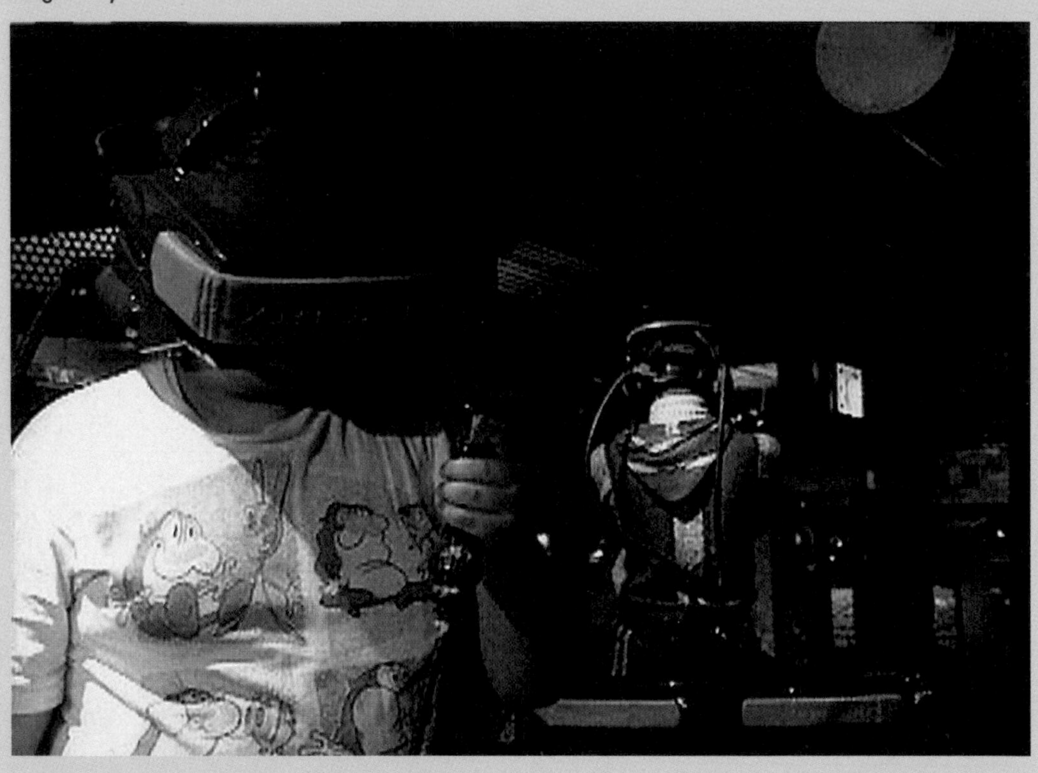

This image was captured from a virtual reality arcade game.

world because sensors report your movements to the computer. The computer then reacts, adjusting the images in response to your actions. Sensors in the HMD track your head movements, so if you turn your head, the scene changes. In some systems, users wear a glove that senses and reports hand movements. Other systems have controls that are like the joysticks used in video games. There are also treadmill devices that let you walk through the virtual world and even a suit that reports body movements to the computer. Advanced systems let several people interact with each other in the same virtual world.

As amazing as they are, VR systems aren't completely realistic. The computer images are often simple and lack fine details. Sometimes there are delays between your actions and the computer's reactions. And you can walk right through a virtual wall. Still, most computer experts expect that the virtual reality experience will become more and more realistic as the imaging technology advances.

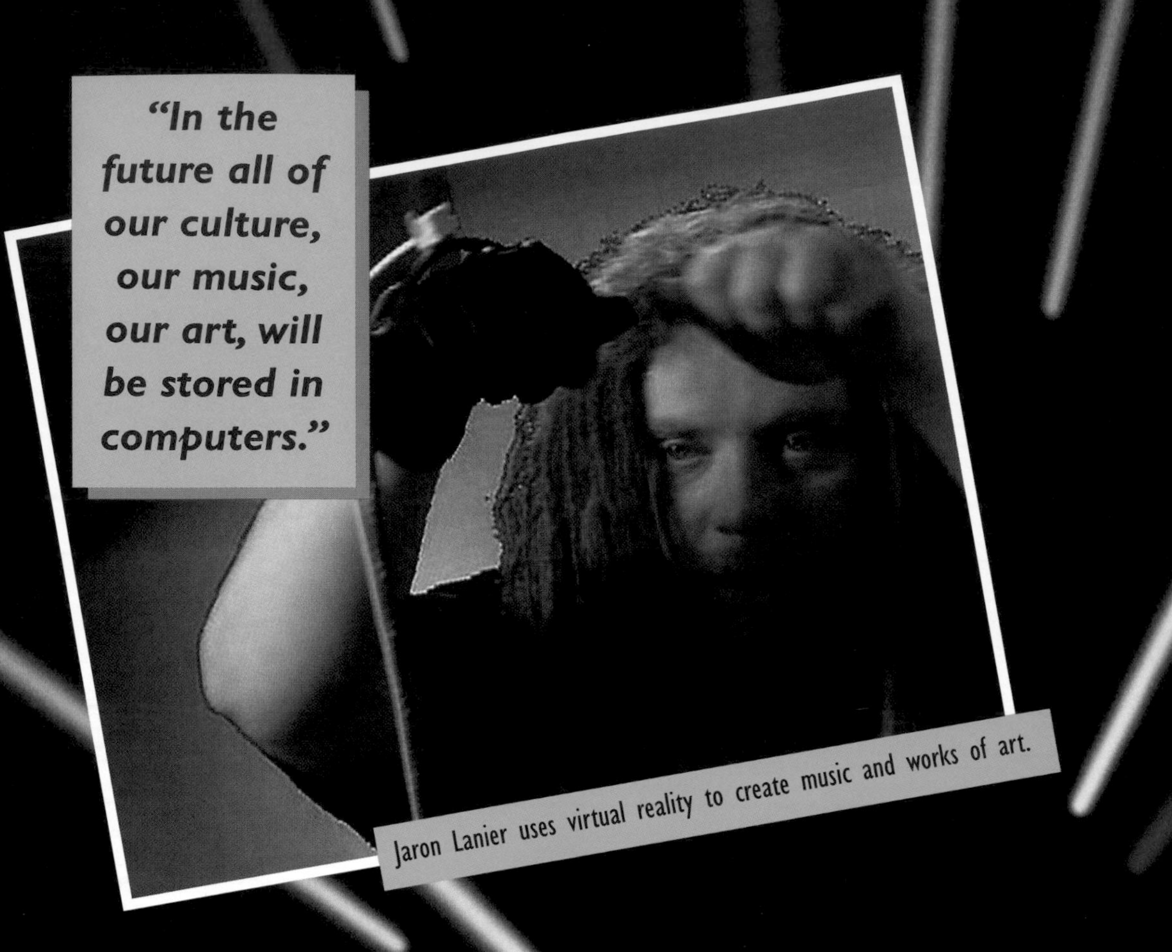

"In the future all of our culture, our music, our art, will be stored in computers."

Jaron Lanier uses virtual reality to create music and works of art.

"Everything about virtual reality that's powerful and beautiful happens because human beings are at the center of the concept and the way it's designed," says Jaron Lanier. "In the future, there will be many cases when people want to design something in the virtual world. How will they do it?" Virtual worlds, Lanier says, are created through a new type of design, a combination of sculpting and computer programming.

Lanier has created a world of musical instruments for the virtual operator to play in a piece he calls "The Sound of One Hand." By moving one hand in the data glove, the operator can touch and play the various instruments. One, the rhythm gimbal, "looks kind of like a gyroscope," Lanier says. "By spinning it in different ways, I can get different qualities of sound." Spinning the rhythm gimbal gently produces soft, eerie background for the other instruments. Among them are a mallet instrument called the cyberxylo, and another called the cybersax.

"The idea is that in the future all of our culture, our music, our writing, our art will be stored in computers. We're going to read literature through computers and see art through computers and hear music through computers. And so it's vital for people to be able to control those computers, for the culture to remain fluid and alive," says Lanier.

Lanier developed a "data glove" wired with sensors that translate hand movements into computer commands.

“Everything about virtual reality that’s powerful and beautiful happens because human beings are at the center of the concept.”

Lanier believes computers can eventually be used to create and explore nearly all aspects of human culture.

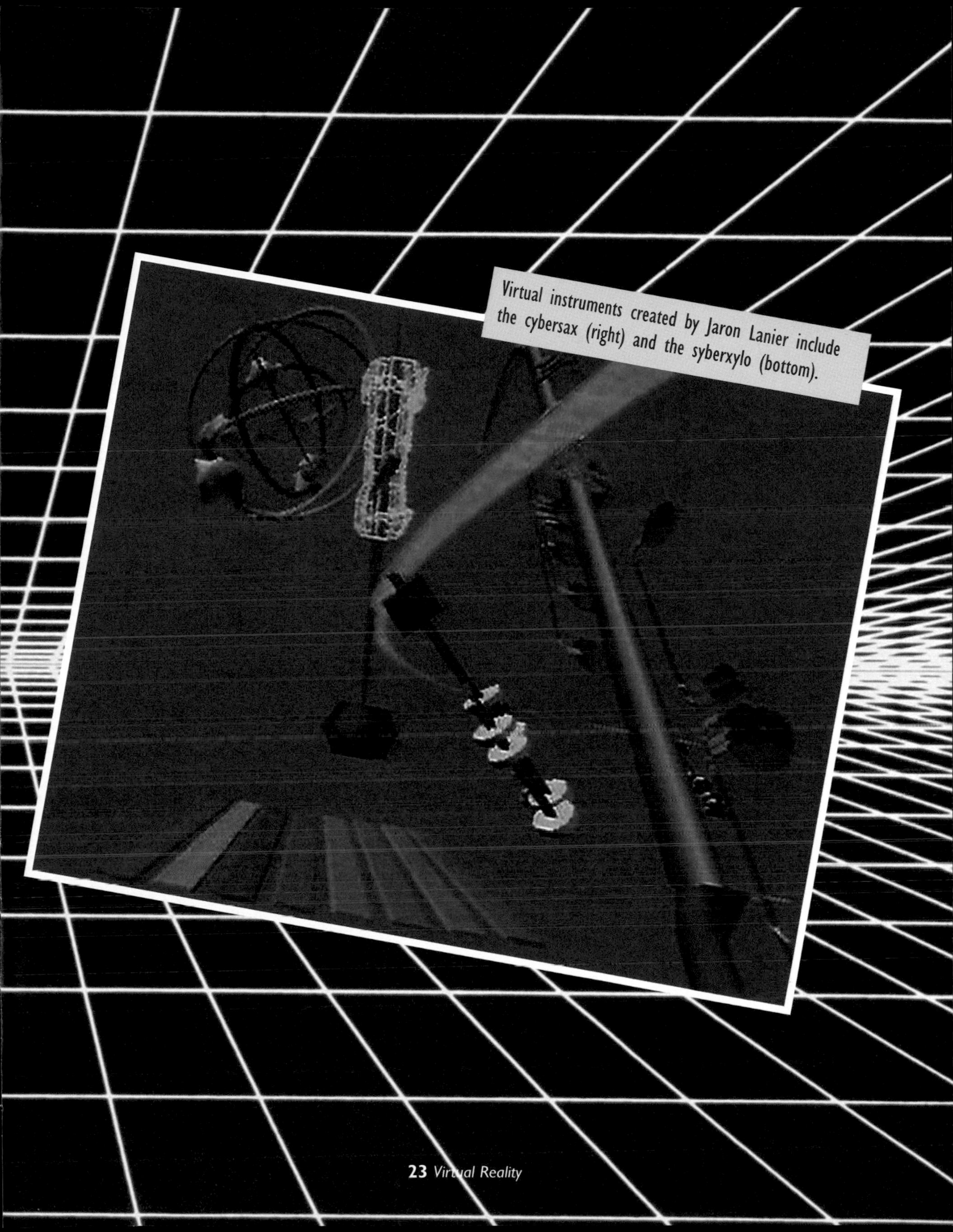

Virtual instruments created by Jaron Lanier include the cybersax (right) and the syberxylo (bottom).

Virtual Promise

What can be done inside virtual reality? That question is being tested and explored all over the world.

The U.S. Air Force came up with a VR simulation to train pilots for bombing missions in the Persian Gulf War. The military has also looked into the possibility of creating a virtual reality helmet that would allow soldiers to locate an enemy's hiding place or identify land mines.

Virtual reality has already been used to train military personnel for combat.

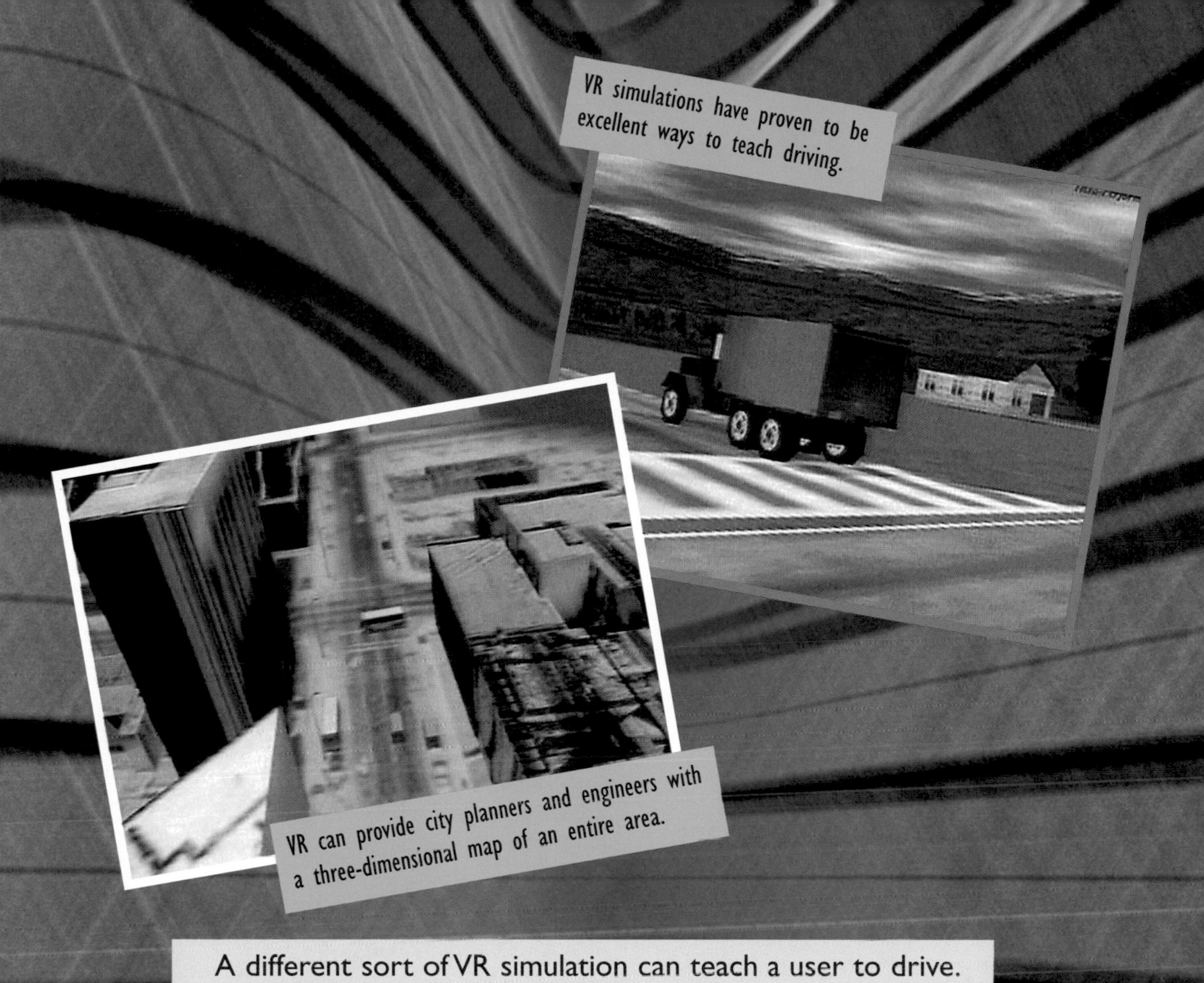
VR simulations have proven to be excellent ways to teach driving.

VR can provide city planners and engineers with a three-dimensional map of an entire area.

A different sort of VR simulation can teach a user to drive. Other vehicles and hazards appear ahead of you as you steer your virtual vehicle down a virtual highway, learning how a car reacts to your controls.

In the Netherlands, another virtual world has been created to teach seamen to navigate inside Rotterdam Harbor, one of the busiest shipping ports in the world.

City planners in Minneapolis, Minnesota, came up with a three-dimensional map of the downtown area. It can be used to view streets at ground level, or to see an entire area in an aerial view. If someone wants to construct a building, planners can see in an instant how it will affect the city.

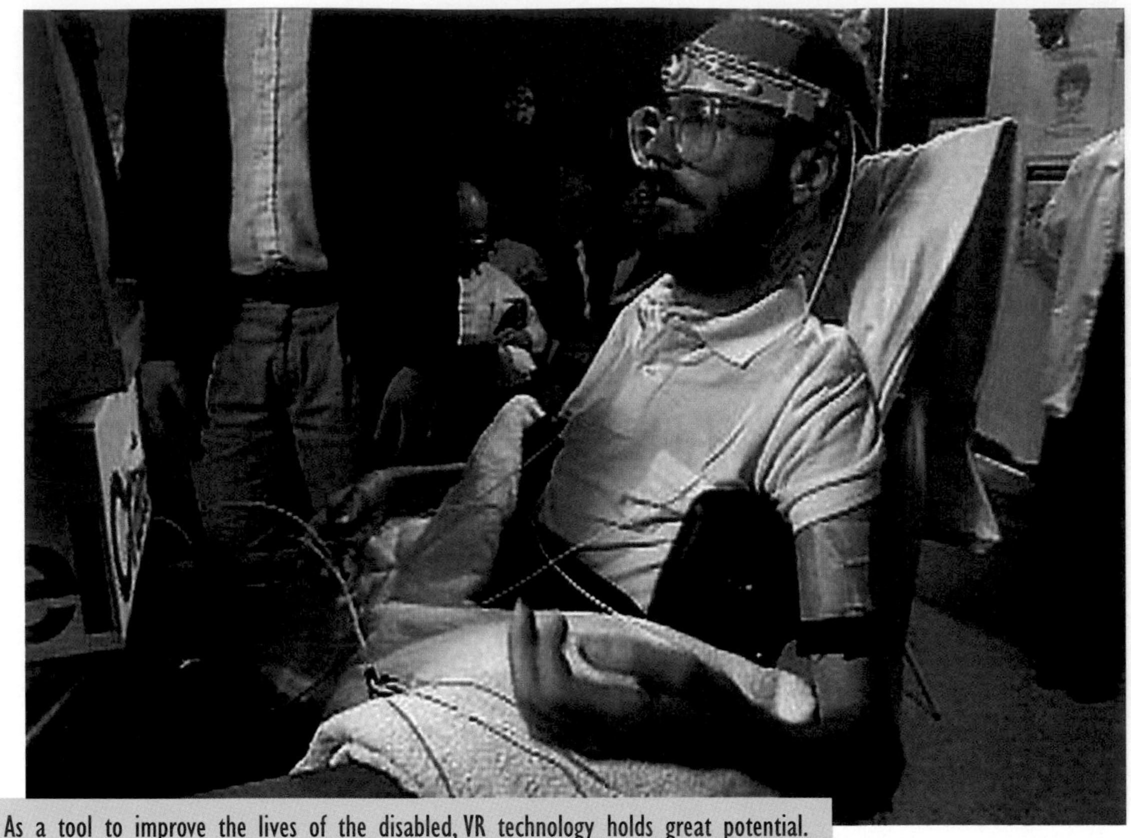
As a tool to improve the lives of the disabled, VR technology holds great potential.

Among the most promising uses being explored are ways in which virtual reality may be able to help the disabled. The hope is that virtual reality will one day allow disabled people to speak, turn on lights, switch on call buttons for nurses, turn on heaters, even play music.

UNC is working on its own contributions to medicine of the future, including a head-mounted display for surgeons. Such displays might be used for needle biopsies, in which a surgeon uses a needle to draw out a bit of body tissue to determine if cancer is present.

These sketches show how VR may one day enable surgeons to "see" inside their patients and to transmit the images to others all over the world.

Fuchs explains, "The surgeon wearing a head-mounted display would be able to see into the patient as she thrusts the needle in to get a sample of cells from a deep tumor." The system would also allow the surgeon to consult with another doctor during the procedure—even a doctor thousands of miles away. Computer-scanned images of the patient could be sent to the consultant, who would view them through a head-mounted display or a standard computer work station.

"It's an exceedingly promising, exciting technology," says UNC's Fred Brooks. But, he cautions, "The hype occasionally outruns the reality. I'm very concerned that the field has had so much hype. It leads people to believe that we're promising things we can't deliver or that we're promising things we may be able to deliver in ten years."

Dr. Brooks forsees VR applications in nearly all aspects of daily life.

"It's an exceedingly promising, exciting technology," says Dr. Brooks.

VIRTUAL FUN

Virtual reality is the latest thing in video games—and VR games aren't at all like standard video games. Virtual reality immerses players completely in the game world, so that they're not aware of the real world. And these games are fully interactive. Players not only control the action, but what they see changes with their movements. Here are some examples:

- *BATTLE TECH: In this ten-minute game for up to eight players, you're a robot—a Mech—fighting other Mechs, who are the other players. You can battle on your own or form teams with other players, plotting strategy by microphone during the game.*
- *CYBERGATE: You put on a VR helmet and take the controls of your own spacecraft in a virtual battle with other craft, piloted by other players.*
- *DACTYLE NIGHTMARE: Wearing a VR helmet, you search through a weird virtual world. You've got to find the bad guys (the other players) before they find you—and before the evil pterodactyl that's circling overhead swoops down to carry you off.*
- *R360: This game combines virtual reality with the excitement of an amusement park ride. You sit in the cockpit of a spacecraft, strap on a VR display, and take off. As you put your craft through turns and rolls, your virtual view changes—and the cockpit actually twirls and tumbles.*

VR equipment is very expensive, so most true virtual reality games are designed for arcades rather than homes. Home versions of VR equipment may become more affordable as the technology improves. At that point, virtual reality may create a real revolution in entertainment.

VIRTUAL HERE AND NOW

One thing that virtual reality can deliver to the consumer today—besides new and more "realistic" video games—is a new way to build and decorate homes. In fact, the Japanese are already using virtual reality to take prospective buyers on "tours" of new homes. And Autodesk, a software development company in Sausalito, California, is using virtual reality to take the idea of a blueprint to a completely new level. With their technology, people can see inside homes that have not yet been built. They can also change the elements of that home with an almost infinite number of options at their disposal.

In a virtual house plan, all the lines are drawn in the same way that they would be if an architect were to prepare plans for the building. But the view is three dimensional, and you can "walk into it." If you want to build or remodel a house, you can enter a virtual house that's been created just for you. Before construction even begins, you can see where the windows or the kitchen cabinets would go, and try out different designs, colors, and arrangements.

Bill Kurtis gets suited up for a VR experience.

"I feel as if I'm really in a kitchen."

Bill Kurtis "walks through" a virtual kitchen.

Using such a system at UNC, Bill Kurtis entered a virtual reality kitchen. Ahead of him was a stove, with a frying pan on it and counters and cabinets around it. The refrigerator was on the far wall. As he virtual "walked" through the kitchen, he got a sense of how the work space was laid out—and how to rearrange it to make it better.

The virtual world of the kitchen is much closer to the real world than the sea of molecules Bill had entered previously. This time, Bill says: "It's not moving and changing around me, and I don't feel weightless. I feel as if I'm really in a kitchen—in fact, I begin to feel hungry."

Dr. Brooks explains that he's had similar experiences. "I find that after I've been in the imaginary kitchen for about 20 or 30 minutes, I'm surprised to be back in the laboratory when I come out. There's a little bit of an emotional shock."

Virtual kitchens such as this enable architects, designers, and homeowners to work with limitless possibilites before deciding on a final design.

"Being able to visualize the molecule tells us a lot about its physical properties."

Stan Williams has developed technology to help chemists visualize molecular structures.

"Virtual" molecules show scientists the actual structures of materials.

Incredible Shrinking People

The virtual kitchen was fun, but the real challenge for the UNC lab was to see how virtual reality could help scientists take their work into a new dimension. And the opportunity to test the UNC system came from Dr. Stan Williams, a materials scientist at the University of California at Los Angeles and an old college friend of Warren Robinett's.

"Chemists are well known for building models of the substances we look at," Williams says. "We do this to see how the atoms are arranged and how the molecules are structured. That helps for a lot of reasons. Being able to visualize the molecule tells us a lot about its physical properties—its strength, for example—and the way it will behave, including how it takes part in chemical reactions."

Williams wanted to be able to study the structure of molecules in minute detail. So he built a device called a scanning tunneling microscope. The device doesn't work like a traditional optical microscope, in which you look through a lens and see something that has been magnified. Instead, it uses an electrical current to map the surface of the object being studied.

"It's more like a Braille microscope," Williams explains. "A tip moves back and forth across the surface of the sample that you're looking at, and you monitor the amount of electrical current flowing between the tip and the sample." The current varies as the surface changes. A computer can create an image of the surface by taking the data about the current and mapping it on screen.

Williams's scanning tunneling microscope.

The scanning tunneling microscope allowed Williams to see molecules on an atomic scale. To get a sense of this scale, imagine that you can view the United States from space, from a point so far away that the entire country is the size of your thumb. Then suppose that you can spot a postage stamp somewhere in the country. Now you have an idea of the detail the scanning tunneling microscope can provide.

All the same, the images produced by the microscope didn't give Williams the detail he needed. So he called Robinett, his old college friend. The UNC team went into action. They hooked Williams's microscope up to their VR system. They came up with a name for the new device—the nanomanipulator. And they started looking around.

With the nanomanipulator, the scientists could be transported down to the surface of a substance they wanted to study, like incredible shrinking people in a science-fiction film. Something that measured a nanometer—1 billionth of a meter—across was suddenly 2 feet (.60 meter) wide! The molecular structure of a substance like graphite appeared in incredible detail, with peaks and valleys that the scientists had never seen before.

"I think of it as a computer enhancement of my senses," Williams says. "When I'm on the nanomanipulator, I can scale myself down, and atoms become the size of basketballs. I can run my hand over the surface and actually feel the atoms. I can see and experience them firsthand, something I just can't do in any other fashion."

The nanomanipulator puts the chemist down on a virtual surface—a model that's as close to the real thing as the instruments can make it. It takes the measurements produced by the microscope and puts them in a form that people can see. And that makes the information easier to understand and remember.

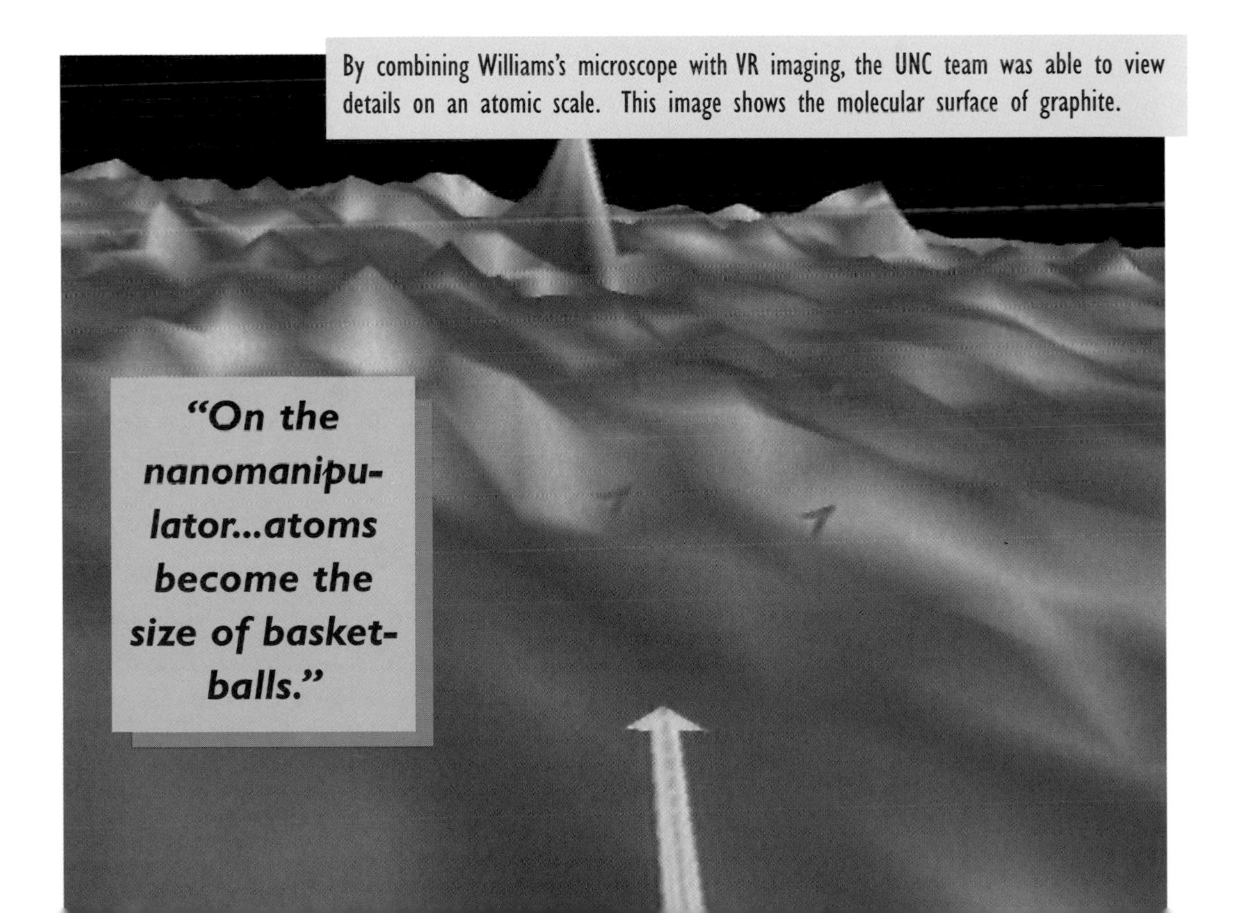

By combining Williams's microscope with VR imaging, the UNC team was able to view details on an atomic scale. This image shows the molecular surface of graphite.

"On the nanomanipulator...atoms become the size of basketballs."

Dr. Stan Williams: Chemistry with Reality

"It was pretty much of a leap of faith on my part to take down a working scientific instrument like the scanning tunneling microscope, put it on an airplane to North Carolina, and have it set up in someone else's lab, so they could work on it and try it out," remembers Stan Williams. "I might never see it again. But, no guts, no glory—I had to give it a shot."

Shipping the instrument coast to coast turned out to be well worth the risk. The nanomanipulator, created by combining the microscope with the UNC virtual reality system, "gives chemistry a reality that even I hadn't appreciated before," Williams says. "I can reach out and touch an atom, and think of being able to pick it up and move it—of doing chemistry one atom at a time. I think this idea is going to completely change the science of chemistry."

"I can reach out and touch an atom."

LIFE THROUGH THE LOOKING GLASS

Other scientists are beginning to see how they can use virtual reality to explore objects that are too small to see in the real world. And virtual reality is helping people travel through space, to explore distant planets. The surface of Venus has been mapped by an unmanned spacecraft, and at the National Aeronautics and Space Administration (NASA), the information has been fed into a computer. For the first time, scientists are able to visualize the cloud-covered surface of the planet.

Computer-generated graphics show scientists what the surfaces of distant planets, such as Venus, are like.

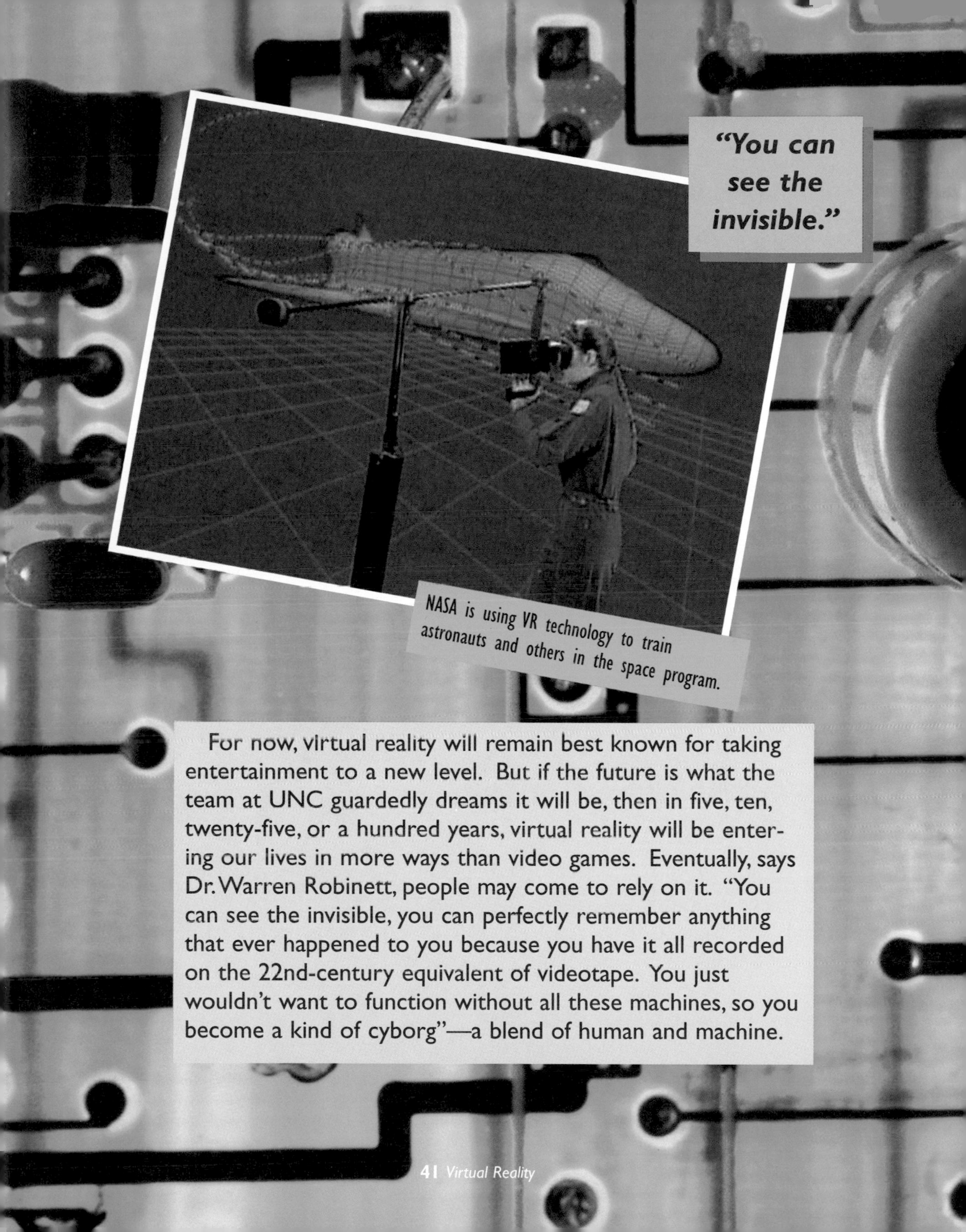

NASA is using VR technology to train astronauts and others in the space program.

For now, virtual reality will remain best known for taking entertainment to a new level. But if the future is what the team at UNC guardedly dreams it will be, then in five, ten, twenty-five, or a hundred years, virtual reality will be entering our lives in more ways than video games. Eventually, says Dr. Warren Robinett, people may come to rely on it. "You can see the invisible, you can perfectly remember anything that ever happened to you because you have it all recorded on the 22nd-century equivalent of videotape. You just wouldn't want to function without all these machines, so you become a kind of cyborg"—a blend of human and machine.

VIRTUALLY THERE

Fly over the surface of Mars, zooming around mountains and diving into valleys for a close look. Visit the deepest trenches of the ocean. Explore an active volcano crater that's filled with poisonous gases. One day, you may be able to do all these things in perfect safety—through the magic of virtual reality.

Visiting places through virtual reality is sometimes called telepresence. Telepresence begins with measurements and other information gleaned by scientific instruments. The information is fed into a computer, which uses data to create three-dimensional images. Then, with the help of a VR display, you can drop in for a virtual visit.

By combining virtual reality with robots, people can do more than look around. For example, virtual reality is taking scientists to the bottom of the ocean. A robot explores inaccessible regions and collects samples under the sea. Its operator uses a VR system to view images transmitted by the robot and to control the robot's actions.

Scientists at NASA are developing a system that could be used on live missions to distant worlds such as Mars. A remote-controlled rover could explore the Martian surface, sending information and images back to a VR system at a safe base. There, astronauts could view VR images and control the rover—telling it to stop to check out something interesting, or to pick up some particular rock samples that appear useful.

Or, instead of going on a dangerous "space walk," an astronaut may be able to send a robot into space to repair a satellite. Wearing a VR helmet and data gloves, the astronaut could view images relayed by the robot. She would "repair" the satellite in virtual reality. The VR system would monitor her arm and hand motions and tell the robot to mimic them.

Similar VR systems may one day be used in many dangerous situations. VR-guided robots could clean up toxic wastes, repair nuclear reactors, and perform other high-risk but necessary jobs.

Dr. Henry Fuchs imagines a day when people will carry around their own personal VR systems, in the form of eyeglass-mounted displays the size of postage stamps and Walkman-size computers that clip onto belts. Stored in the computer would be a wealth of information—encyclopedias, dictionaries, stacks of photographs—thousands of topics stored over the years. Wherever you went, you would have access to that data, and the ability to create your own three-dimensional world.

Dr. Fuchs believes VR can eventually be adapted for individual and personal use.

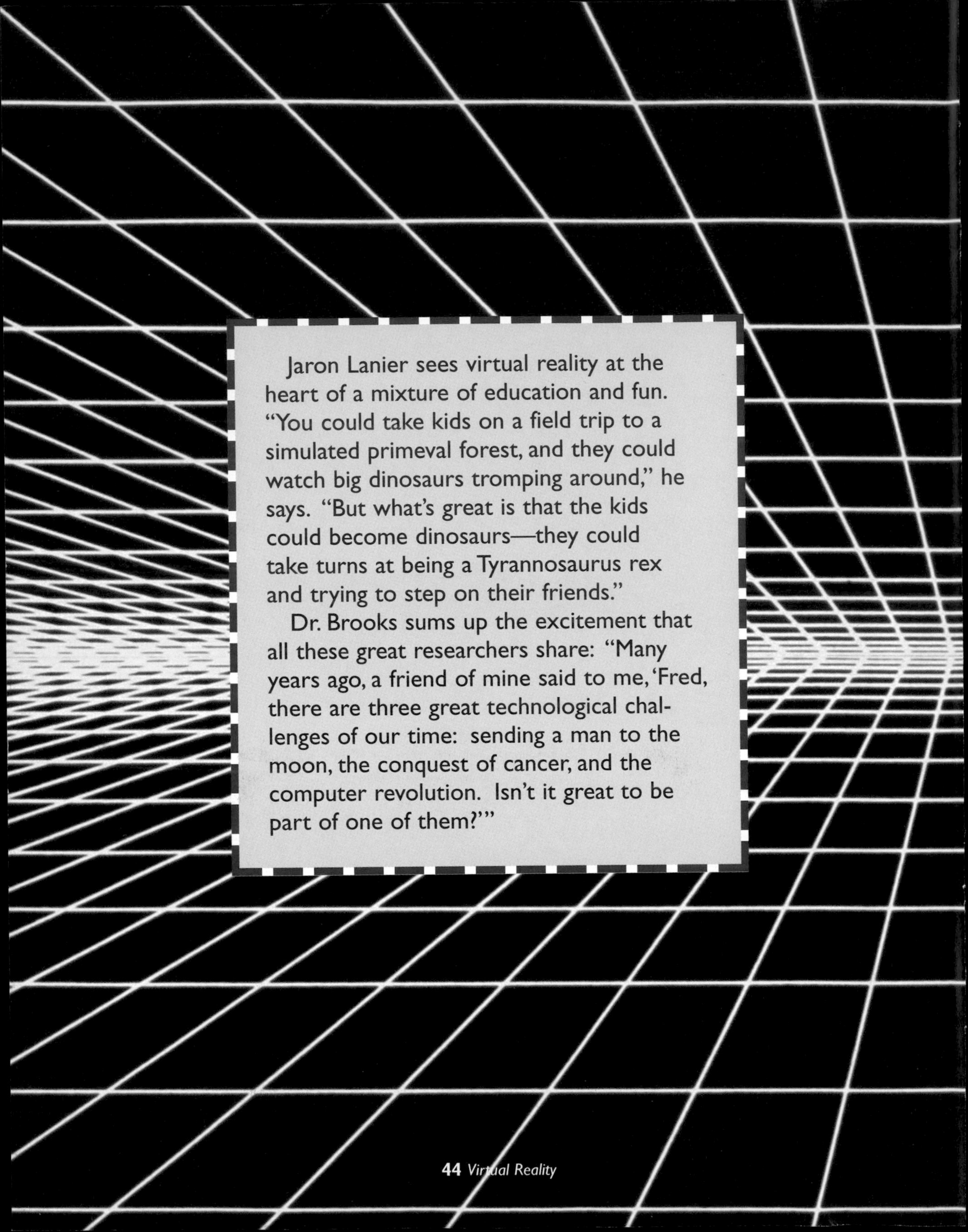

Jaron Lanier sees virtual reality at the heart of a mixture of education and fun. "You could take kids on a field trip to a simulated primeval forest, and they could watch big dinosaurs tromping around," he says. "But what's great is that the kids could become dinosaurs—they could take turns at being a Tyrannosaurus rex and trying to step on their friends."

Dr. Brooks sums up the excitement that all these great researchers share: "Many years ago, a friend of mine said to me, 'Fred, there are three great technological challenges of our time: sending a man to the moon, the conquest of cancer, and the computer revolution. Isn't it great to be part of one of them?'"

Students at UNC's computer research facility work on developing the next wave of VR breakthroughs.

Glossary

atom The smallest particle of a chemical element.

cyborg A human being whose abilities are enhanced by electronic devices.

gimbal A ringlike support that allows an object to turn in any direction.

interactive Involving two-way communication, as when a computer reacts to your commands.

molecule The smallest complete particle of a substance. Molecules are made up of atoms.

real time The actual time during which something happens.

Further Reading

Atelsek, Jean. *All About Computers.* Emeryville, CA: Ziff-Davis, 1993.

Billings, Charlene W. *Supercomputers: Shaping the Future.* New York: Facts On File, 1995.

Borman, Jami Lynne. *Computer Dictionary for Kids...and Their Parents.* Hauppauge, NY: Barron's, 1995.

Bortz, Alfred B. *Mind Tools: The Science of Artificial Intelligence.* New York: Franklin Watts, 1992.

Smith, Norman F. and Douglas W. *Simulators.* New York: Franklin Watts, 1989.

Weiss, Ann E. Virtual Reality: *A Door to Cyperspace.* New York: Twenty-First Century, 1996.

Web Sites

http://www.pbs.org/wttw/web_newexp/
The official homepage of The New Explorers television series. Lists the show broadcast schedule, educational resources, and information about how to join The New Explorers Club as well as how to participate in The New Explorers electronic field trip.

http://www.cs.unc.edu/
Find out more about the Virtual Reality projects going on at University of North Carolina at their homepage.

http://www.well.com/user/jaron/
The website of Jaron Lanier, the Virtual Reality pioneer in art and music—includes samples of his artwork, writings, and schedule of personal appearances.

http://198.93.152.12/index.html
Autodesk's homepage—Learn about cutting-edge Virtual Reality products, 3D Careers, and visit their "virtual campus."

http://www.jsc.nasa.gov
The homepage of the Johnson Space Center/NASA—learn more about how NASA uses virtual reality for testing; resources for educators and kids.

http://www.vrs.org.uk/
The Virtual Reality Society website—features a searchable database of Virtual Reality companies and an online glossary of over 500 Virtual Reality related terms.

Index

Photo Credits
Page 3: Bill Arnold
Pages 23, 25: Will Crockett